C-
921
Wy

Sandak

First Families:the Washingtons
31502

DATE DUE

JUN 13, 2018

PRINTED IN U.S.A.

The
Washingtons

by
Cass R. Sandak

CRESTWOOD HOUSE
New York

Maxwell Macmillan Canada
Toronto

Maxwell Macmillan International
New York   Oxford   Singapore   Sydney

Library of Congress Cataloging-in-Publication Data
Sandak, Cass R.
   The Washingtons / by Cass R. Sandak. — 1st ed.
      p.   cm. — (First families)
   Includes bibliographical references and index.
   Summary: An account of the life of George Washington and his family, with emphasis on his years as president.
   ISBN 0-89686-635-1
   1. Washington, George, 1732–1799—Juvenile literature. 2. Washington, George, 1732–1799—Family—Juvenile
literature. 3. Washington family—Juvenile literature. 4. Presidents—United States—Biography—Juvenile
literature. 5. United States—Politics and government—1789–1797—Juvenile literature. [1. Washington, George,
1732–1799. 2. Presidents. 3. Washington, Martha, 1731–1802. 4. First ladies.] I. Title. II. Series.
E312.66.S26   1991
973.4′1′0922—dc20   91-6700
[B]   CIP
                                                                                                              AC

Photo Credits
Cover: National Gallery of Art
The Bettmann Archive: 4, 7, 9, 15, 16, 19, 21, 23, 25, 26, 27, 29, 31, 35, 41, 43
National Gallery of Art: 10
Library of Congress: 32
Historical Society of Pennsylvania: 38

Copyright © 1991 Crestwood House, Macmillan Publishing Company

Macmillan Publishing Company   Maxwell Macmillan Canada, Inc.
866 Third Avenue   1200 Eglinton Avenue East
New York, NY 10022   Suite 200
                                        Don Mills, Ontario M3C 3N1

CRESTWOOD HOUSE

Macmillan Publishing Company is part of the Maxwell Communication Group of Companies.

Produced by Flying Fish Studio

Printed in the United States of America

First edition

10 9 8 7 6 5 4 3 2 1

CONTENTS

The inauguration of George Washington as the first President of the United States, on the balcony of Old City Hall, April 30, 1789

The First Inauguration

It was a Thursday and the place was New York City, then the young nation's capital. The date was April 30 and the year was 1789. George Washington had traveled up the East River in a noisy procession of boats and cannon. He now stood on a balcony outside Federal Hall on Wall Street.

With his hand on the Bible, Washington took an oath of office that would make him the first president of the United States. The ceremony taking place was the first inauguration. Washington was 57 years old. He was never an inspired speaker, and on this day he was so nervous that often he could barely be heard.

As the first president, Washington had no tradition to follow. Some people thought that the president should act like a king. Others thought that he should act simply and humbly. After all, the new country was of the people and for the people.

A great deal of what happened would be Washington's doing. He saw his inauguration as the official beginning of his public office. He did not see it as a social occasion. Washington had both a wife and a mother living at the time of the inauguration, but they did not attend the event.

Martha Washington was 58 when her husband was inaugurated as the first president of the United States. In those days travel was difficult. More than that, Martha was needed to manage their estate at Mount Vernon. So Martha remained at home in Virginia until May. Then she joined her husband in New York City. The 200-mile journey from Mount Vernon to New York City by coach took Martha 11 days.

Like her husband, Martha had no tradition to fall back on. In years to come, almost all the presidents' wives would stand beside their husbands as they were sworn in. In fact, Martha did join Washington when he took the oath for his second term of office. By then—March 4, 1793—the event took place in Philadelphia. The Washingtons' adopted children, Nelly and George Washington Parke Custis, were also present. But at that first inauguration, Washington stood alone as he became the country's first president.

After the ceremony, Washington set to work as president of the new nation. And he waited for his family to join him in New York City.

The Young George

George Washington was born on February 22, 1732 at his family's modest farm in Westmoreland County, Virginia. By an old-style calendar then in use, the date was actually February 11. But in 1753 a new calendar was adopted that changed the date to February 22.

Washington leaving New York after his inauguration

George Washington's father was named Augustine. He had married twice, and George was part of his second family. George had no middle name or initial. From the first family came one of George's great friends: his half brother Lawrence. It was from Lawrence that George was to later inherit Mount Vernon.

Augustine married his second wife, Mary Ball, in 1731. George was the eldest of their children. A farmer, Augustine died when George was 11. The family was not aristocratic, but they were well to do.

We don't know much about George Washington's boyhood. When he became famous, it was only natural that people would make up stories about him. One of George's earliest biographers was a Quaker clergyman, Parson Mason L. Weems. He invented the most famous tale of all about the young George. He wrote it in his book, *The Life of Washington*, published in 1806. It now seems unlikely that George ever chopped down the famous cherry tree and then confessed the deed to his father with the words: "Father, I cannot tell a lie."

George was brought up to be a farmer and planter. George was not sent to school in England as his older half brothers had been. Tutors, copybooks and self-study were the basis of the home classroom. His formal education ended when he was about 14. From that time on, everything George knew about manners, morals and practical skills he learned from his family.

After Augustine died, George's mother lived in the comfortable but plain four-room family home on the

*Mary Ball Washington,
George's mother*

Rappahannock River. Later in life, Mary Ball Washington moved into a new house in Fredericksburg, Virginia. Although George frequently visited her there, they were not close. By most accounts, she was a difficult and demanding woman. She never visited Mount Vernon. She spent her days weaving, sewing, knitting and making herbal medicines.

As a young man, Washington was trained as a surveyor. When he was 16, Washington helped survey the Shenandoah Valley for Lord Fairfax, Virginia's greatest landowner. The Shenandoah region was then the western frontier of the British colonies. In 1749 Washington received a surveying license from the College of William and Mary in Williamsburg. This was like receiving a degree in civil engineering today.

Washington was 22 when he was commissioned a lieutenant colonel in 1754. This was the start of the battles that became the French and Indian War. George served as an aide to British Major General Edward Braddock. He rode

beside the general in battle and seemed to lead a charmed life. Bullets pierced his hat and his coat in four places. Two horses were killed while he was riding them. But, riding a third horse, Washington fought on. In ways like this, he became a military hero.

By the time he was an adult, Washington was six feet two inches tall and weighed about 200 pounds. He refused to wear a wig, as was the fashion. Instead he powdered his own hair with chalk.

Throughout his life, Washington suffered from dental problems. He had lost most of his teeth by the time he was middle-aged. He had three pairs of dentures fitted for his mouth. The first set was carved from oak and included eight human teeth inset in it. The second set had been molded from lead. The third set of false teeth Washington had made was carved from hippopotamus ivory. This was his favorite set.

We know what Washington looked like from paintings. He did not, however, like to sit still for artists. We also know from a mask of Washington's face made by a French sculptor. The artist Gilbert Stuart painted the best-known portrait of the first president. The picture shows us how Washington looked when he was about 60 years old. The painting has been on display in the White House since the building was opened in 1800.

A portrait of George Washington by Gilbert Stuart

The Young Martha

Martha "Patsy" Dandridge was born on June 2, 1731. Her birthplace was a plantation on the Pamunkey River not far from Williamsburg, Virginia. Williamsburg was then the capital of the colony of Virginia. Martha was the eldest daughter of John and Frances Dandridge. The family was well off.

Martha was a spirited girl. Today we would probably call her a tomboy. A story is told about how she once rode her horse up the broad front staircase of her uncle's home. She then rode the horse through the entire second floor and down the back stairs!

Like most girls of her time, Martha had little formal education. Sometimes, however, she did take lessons with her younger brothers, who had a tutor from England. Martha always regretted that her education had not been stronger in English grammar and spelling. For this reason she often dictated her letters and then copied them in her own hand. She did learn enough arithmetic to keep her account books straight.

Martha had a keen and quick mind and was an avid reader. Bible readings were part of her daily routine, but she also read other books and what newspapers were available. In this way she kept abreast of happenings in other places.

Like other young ladies of her period and social class, young Martha was brought up to be "accomplished." This meant that she should demonstrate skill in various artistic pursuits. The family's tutor taught her the popular dance steps of the day. A watercolor painting of a butterfly done by Martha shows considerable talent. She was also an expert at needlepoint.

Martha's mother taught her everything a Virginia housewife would have to know: how to manage domestic and plantation servants, how to cook and preserve meats, how to store foods and put up jams, and how to spin, weave and sew.

As a young girl, Martha Dandridge charmed people by her simplicity. By the time she turned 16, Martha was just five feet tall and had wavy brown hair. She had hazel eyes. When Martha was presented to Williamsburg society at her first ball, she was able to hold her own against the town's clever young ladies. Soon after, her well-connected cousins secured her a place at the heart of Williamsburg society.

Martha's First Marriage

Martha married Daniel Parke Custis when she was 17. Custis was considered one of the most eligible men in the colonies. He was heir to possibly the greatest fortune in Virginia. But he was 13 years older than Martha, and the couple had a hard time convincing old Mr. Custis that the match was a good one. Still, Martha's gentle manner won the old man's heart. The girl and her father-in-law were devoted to each other until he died, not long after the marriage.

The Custises lived most of the time at one of the Custis estates. Oddly enough it was called the White House. They also had an impressive mansion in Williamsburg called Six Chimneys.

Daniel and Martha Custis enjoyed only eight years of married life. But the years were happy ones. The couple had four children. Two of them died when they were infants. When Daniel died suddenly in 1757, the two surviving children were both very young. They were a boy named John Parke (Jack) Custis and a girl called Martha Parke (Patty).

When Daniel Custis died, Martha was only 25. She became one of the wealthiest women in the colony of Virginia. Each of the two surviving children also inherited one third of the Custis estate. Their shares were equal to Martha's and were to be held in trust until the children turned 21.

Martha was left with an estate on the James River, several hundred slaves, and 17,000 acres of land planted with tobacco. Tobacco was the great crop of the time. Each year most of the harvest was shipped to London in great wooden casks. In England the tobacco was sold by merchants in an open market. Martha was a smart businesswoman. She demanded that her agents in England command top prices for her crop.

George Washington's first meeting with Martha Custis

George and Martha

The French and Indian War was still going on when George Washington met the young widow Custis. She was very much taken by the tall military officer. She wanted to have a strong man at her side to help manage both her estates and her young children. George was no doubt taken by Martha's charm, not to mention her great wealth.

Less than nine months after her first husband died, Martha was engaged to Colonel Washington. A year and a half later, she was Washington's bride. In colonial times it was expected that a widow—especially a young, rich widow—would remarry. Still, the interval was only a short one. But both Martha and George wanted the wedding to take place soon.

15

The marriage of George Washington and Martha Custis

Martha felt she could hardly make a better second marriage than to the handsome colonel, who was both a successful planter and a renowned soldier.

And George could not hope to find a better—or richer—helpmate than Martha. But Martha was not George's first love. Some years earlier 16-year-old Betsy Fauntleroy, Washington's sweetheart, had turned him down twice.

George and Martha's wedding took place by candlelight in the drawing room of Martha's White House estate. The date was January 6, 1759. Martha was 27 when she and George Washington married. The wedding came at a high point in their lives. In December George had returned home from the French and Indian War with the news that he was retiring from army life.

Little did the Washingtons know that, almost from the start, their marriage would be an unusual one. The demands of duty would call for long periods of separation followed by joyful reunions.

During Washington's absence on the frontier, the citizens of Frederick County had elected him their representative in the Virginia House of Burgesses. George's first speech before the house was a disaster. He merely stood, red-faced and stammering. In later years he became more relaxed in front of crowds, but he was never a great orator.

From 1759 until 1776, when the American Revolution began, the Washingtons lived like a Virginia gentleman and his lady. The household included Martha's children. There were hundreds of slaves to help with the work. Washington could relax, enjoy fox hunts and entertain friends. But he also worked hard to manage the estate.

When George Washington married Martha, he came into possession of whatever Martha owned before the marriage. This was the law in the colonies. In their case, her homes at Six Chimneys and the White House and her tobacco lands, as well as more than $100,000 in cash, were included. George also became guardian of the children's 30,000 acres and $200,000. In addition, he brought more than 5,000 acres of his own property to the marriage.

George and Martha made an interesting contrast as a couple. Martha had a warm and affectionate nature. Washington was a practical, self-possessed man. Some might have considered him cold and unemotional. But he was an efficient soldier and administrator. His sense of duty always came before his own comfort or desires. And he was just the sort of man who knew how to get things done. Washington was the perfect public servant—he always put the wishes of his countrymen ahead of his own.

George and Martha had no children together. It appears that this may have created a certain tension in their marriage. It seems clear from surviving letters that Washington would have preferred to have had heirs of his own.

The Colonies Revolt

As both a military leader and landowner, Washington did not like what was happening to the American colonists under British rule. He was elected a delegate to the Second Continental Congress. This group met in Philadelphia in 1775. Because the British government would not yield to the colonists' demands, war seemed inevitable. A large number of colonists wanted to break away from Great Britain. On July 4, 1776, a war for independence from Great Britain was declared.

Washington had been elected commander in chief of the young American army by the members of the Second Continental Congress. General Washington needed to get his soldiers ready for battle. He was able to organize the men. And he gave them courage and strength to fight the British.

Things began well for Washington. In March 1776 he drove the British out of Boston. By the summer of 1776 he and his troops had moved to New York City. It was there that Washington read the Declaration of Independence to his soldiers. But in August, after the Battle of Long Island, the British successfully kept control of the region. By November the British marched into New Jersey. They used German troops to fortify the town of Trenton.

On the cold Christmas night of 1776, some of Washington's men crossed the ice-clogged Delaware River. They swiftly and silently marched toward Trenton, where they surprised the Germans and won a great victory. Ten days later Washington and his remaining troops had won New Jersey for the colonies. But the tide turned later in 1777: They lost Philadelphia and went into retreat at nearby Valley Forge. Although the French joined American forces in 1779, the army was getting smaller and weaker. The

Washington crossing the Delaware River

fighting dragged on. But finally, in 1781, the last battle occurred. Washington and his men were victorious over the British general Cornwallis at Yorktown, Virginia.

A few months after Washington had taken command, in 1775, Martha joined her husband and his soldiers. She spent part of every winter with him during the long, hard years of the war. There had been rumors during the Revolutionary War that Martha was a Tory, or British loyalist. But the rumors were just that.

The war years saw Martha's popularity increase, especially because she spent so much time near the troops. She was with the troops at Trenton and later during the cold, harsh winter at Valley Forge. She helped to nurse the sick. She made bandages for the wounded. At Valley Forge, one regiment named itself "Lady Washington's Dragoons."

By 1781 the war was over and independence had been won. It would be two more years until a peace treaty was signed. The new country did not have a leader. And it had no rules for governing.

Just before Christmas in 1783, Washington resigned his position as head of the army. Once more he returned to Mount Vernon. There he and Martha hoped to live a quiet life.

Life at Mount Vernon

Throughout their lives, George and Martha were early risers. George began his day at 4 A.M. He would go over the accounts of their extensive estates. At 7:30 he breakfasted

Washington directing the workers on his Mount Vernon plantation

on tea, honey and hoe (corn) cakes. He ate sparingly because he wanted to keep his slim military figure. By 8 o'clock George was usually mounted on his horse and off on a daily tour of inspection. He had to see that everything was running smoothly.

The Mount Vernon estate was organized into five farms. Hundreds of black and white laborers raised crops mainly of wheat and tobacco. Many slaves were needed to keep the plantation running well. Martha was up early too, organizing the slaves' work in and around the house. She had to see that their orders were clear and that they had enough supplies. She also had to see that new slaves were properly trained.

After her early-morning refreshment, Martha retired to her room to read the Bible for an hour. She kept up this practice throughout her life. She believed it gave her the strength to get through the day.

Martha was accustomed to having servants to help with the endless chores, both inside and outside the house. But she managed to run her home without the aid of a housekeeper until 1784.

If her children were home, Martha joined them for a more substantial breakfast of ham and hoecakes. She was especially fond of tea and buns called Sally Lunns. These light, fluffy cakes originally came from Bath, a fashionable English resort town. Martha was not careful about her figure and relied more on tight corsets than diet control.

A capable housewife, Martha was responsible for keeping the larder well stocked with dried and preserved fruits. Mount Vernon's beautiful orchards supplied peaches and apples, cherries and plums. Some were dried, some were boiled into preserves, and some were put in jars with brandy or other spirits.

An American plantation was an almost completely self-sufficient place. This means that the plantation supplied nearly all the food and clothing for master, mistress and their children, as well as for staff, gardeners and field hands.

Silk cloth and lace were imported from Europe. Many elegant furnishings came from England—until the colonists began to revolt and refused to import goods from England. Bed and table linens had to be woven and stitched. Only occasionally was wool, linen or cotton cloth purchased. Usually it was produced on the plantation. Fibers were separated, spun into threads and woven into cloth.

When the Washingtons were living at Mount Vernon, George would return from his daily inspections by

midafternoon. He changed from riding clothes into a clean shirt, shoes and stockings. Then the family dinner was served around three o'clock.

Martha excelled at menu planning and enjoyed making guests feel at home. She was a superb cook and was especially proud of her rich cakes and custards. Martha created the recipes for many of Washington's favorite foods: Smithfield ham with oyster sauce, mashed sweet potatoes with coconut, cream of peanut soup, and whiskey cake.

Martha was so lavish in her use of dairy products that the Washingtons sometmes had to buy additional butter and cream from nearby farms. Their own dairy of a hundred cows could not supply enough. And there was a steady stream of guests to be fed.

Following dinner there was plenty of time for additional pursuits. If there was enough daylight, Martha often worked for a few hours in the garden. George usually went over his overseers' reports and wrote up the estate's accounts in his ledgers. Sometimes he read books on farming methods. Books about agriculture and collections of poetry also formed part of the extensive library in the Washington home.

Early evening brought the last meal of the day. This was often a light supper of tea and toast, unless there were guests, when the meal would be more substantial. When there was company, entertainment might include songs at the piano or card games. George enjoyed music, but he never learned to play the flute that he kept in the music room at Mount Vernon.

Washington dancing the minuet with Sally Fairfax

Frequent guests included the Fairfaxes and members of other distinguished Virginia families. George William and Sally Fairfax were probably the Washingtons' closest friends. Their beautiful estate, Belvoir, was about two miles down the Potomac River. The Fairfaxes came to have dinner and spend the night about twice a week. And the Washingtons dined with them just as often.

Sally Fairfax was one of the most cultivated women in the colonies. Washington had been infatuated by her since he was a youth. And there is some evidence that Martha was jealous—rightly or wrongly—of George's feelings for Sally. The intelligent, well-read and sophisticated Sally was two years older than George. She had taught him how to dance and how to act in polite society. They remained close friends throughout their lives, even after Sally and her husband moved to England.

The Mount Vernon Yule log

Christmas with the Washingtons

The Washingtons were typical Virginia planters. They kept Christmas in the Virginia tradition. They were Anglicans (members of the Church of England) and followed the customs of Christmas joy and merrymaking that had been brought to Virginia by the first English settlers. Visitors and friends were welcomed. Food was plentiful. George loved eggnog. And Martha's recipe for a great Christmas cake called for 40 eggs!

The Washingtons celebrated the full Christmas season, from Christmas Eve to Twelfth Night (January 6). In fact, George and Martha were married on Twelfth Night. Games, fox hunting, singing and dancing were all part of the merriment.

26

Washington had had his share of hard Christmases. On Christmas night in 1776 he had rowed across the Delaware River. With his soldiers, he was on the way to win a major battle in the Revolutionary War. And in 1777 he and his men passed the difficult winter at Valley Forge. But Martha had been at his side. That year, in place of Christmas cakes and pies, the Washingtons had served up potatoes, cabbage and turnips to the frostbitten soldiers.

In 1783 Washington returned to Mount Vernon shortly before Christmas. He had visited his home only once during the previous eight years. The plantation was ready for the holiday, decked with holly, mistletoe and evergreens. On Christmas Day a yule log burned in the main fireplace. All the rooms were bright with candles and cheery fires.

Christmas Eve at Mount Vernon

Visitors came to exchange holiday greetings. The Washingtons' slaves were the first to call, eager to receive their traditional Christmas gifts from their mistress's own hand. This was usually some small, useful item, such as a length of fabric to be made into clothing.

Christmas 1789 found President and Mrs. Washington attending services at St. Paul's Church in Manhattan. It is said that Washington's favorite Christmas hymn was "While Shepherds Watch Their Flocks by Night."

Duty Calls Once More

The years following the peace treaty with England in 1783 were among the happiest for George and Martha. Home again, they set about restoring the house and estate to its former prosperity. Overgrown fields were once more cultivated and sown. Fences were mended. New gardens were laid out and new outbuildings were built. Inside the house everything was cleaned and polished, painted and repaired. The Washingtons never expected to have to leave their beloved Mount Vernon again.

But in 1787 duty brought Washington back into public life. The Constitutional Convention met in that year in Philadelphia. Men from all over the country gathered there to form a set of rules to govern the new nation. Washington was chosen president of the convention. After four months of duty he was free to go back to Mount Vernon.

The signing of the Constitution

29

This freedom did not last long. In February 1789 Washington was inspecting his fields at Mount Vernon when Charles Thomson arrived. He had an important message: Washington had just been chosen first president of the United States!

Washington had refused any salary during his eight years as head of the Continental army. As a result, by the time the war was over he needed money. Although the president's salary was small, he accepted it.

The country was small, too, and it was poor. The army and navy were weak. And the Constitution was new. It had not yet been tested.

One of the provisions of the new Constitution was the electoral college. It was this body that had unanimously made Washington the first president.

Washington gave authority to his department heads. In later years these people were called the "cabinet." Washington let these men discuss important issues. This meant that they had a great deal of control.

Some people felt that Washington was not a strong leader because he gave so much power to his helpers. And Washington himself was a slow and deliberate person.

John Adams had been elected vice president. This position, then as now, was second in command to the president. If something should happen to the president, a vice president would know what to do. Because Washington and Adams were not friendly, the two men ignored each other and didn't really work together.

Washington could be an intimidating character. People who knew him and strangers often felt uncomfortable in his

George Washington with the first cabinet members

presence. The liveliness of Martha Washington, "always good humored and cheerful," went a long way toward putting most people at ease. But George Washington was known to drive a hard bargain, never paying too much for anything —a piece of land, a pair of carriage horses, or some breeding stock.

Washington found ceremonies a burden. The life of a squire at Mount Vernon came more easily to him than the role of president.

Washington was 57 when he again left Mount Vernon to resume a place in public life. In April 1789 he set off by coach to New York for the inauguration.

Three weeks later, Martha and her grandchildren were on their way to New York. They went by coach and made several stops along the way. They stopped to see Eleanor, Martha's daughter-in-law, the widow of her son John Custis. She was the mother of little Nelly and George Washington Parke Custis. These were the two grandchildren George and Martha had adopted after John Custis died. Nelly was ten years old and Washington was eight when they traveled with their grandmother. The little group also made stops in Philadelphia and in New Jersey.

The first presidential home, Governor House, in New York

The Washingtons in New York

While they were in New York City, Martha, George and the children lived in a three-story brick house. Number 10 Cherry Street was the presidential "palace." But it was far from grand.

The house and its furnishings had been rented from Samuel Osgood. He had just been appointed postmaster general. To make the house feel more like home, the Washingtons brought some things from Mount Vernon. These included a large portrait of Louis XVI, a gift from the French king.

Martha had a staff who helped her plan parties. The president was host at receptions on Tuesdays. Martha was in charge of dinners on Thursdays and tea parties on Fridays.

Martha had been reared to have a cheerful disposition and to be able to laugh in the face of adversity. She never gave in to despair, and her courage helped to give George Washington strength. But in New York her gentle temperament was stretched. She hated their life there and referred to this time as her "lost days." She would much rather have been home at Mount Vernon.

Martha liked to think of herself as an "old-fashioned Virginia housekeeper—busy as a bee, regular as a clock, and cheerful as a cricket."

The Washingtons had to set their own style as the first family during these years. It was necessary, as head of state, for the first president to show some formality. It was important to impress visitors from the grand courts of Europe. They had to see that the United States was a civilized place, and that Americans were cultivated and well-mannered people. But the Washingtons also had their own relaxed, more American, style of entertaining.

Some people criticized the Washingtons for being too simple in their social life. But others accused them of pretending to be royalty. Martha was hurt by a letter from David Stuart, her daughter-in-law Eleanor's second husband. Stuart wrote that rumors had reached them in Virginia saying her receptions were "awkward imitations of royalty" and that she was "distant and stiff."

Martha frequently appeared at elegant balls with her

own hair simply dressed. Not for her the elaborately curled and powdered wigs that were the fashion of the time. She was a thrifty and practical housewife. It did not matter to Martha if her gowns were adorned with scraps of lace or satin cut from old gowns. Or if a panel of drapery found itself recycled into a sturdy garment. It has been said that she even unraveled the thread in her old gowns and re-wound it on spools!

Occasionally Martha's way of dressing annoyed some high-society ladies. They thought the first lady should always be in the height of fashion. Some humbler people thought Martha and the whole Washington household were too fancy for leaders of a democracy. But through it all, Martha was always herself.

The lives of the Washingtons are well known to us. We know what they thought and how they felt about many things. From relatively young ages they kept diaries and journals that have come down to us. In those days before telephones, everyone wrote letters. Many of the Washingtons' letters have survived, even though late in life Martha destroyed much of their personal correspondence. She did not want their letters to be read by strangers after she and her husband were dead.

In a letter that does survive, she wrote to her friend Mercy Warren in Boston: "I am still determined to be cheerful and happy in whatever situation I may be. For I have also learned from experience that the greater part of our happiness, or misery, depends on our dispositions and not on our circumstances. We carry the seeds of the one or the other about with us in our minds wherever we go."

34   *George and Martha with Martha Parke Custis
          and John Parke Custis*

As the president's wife, Martha was referred to as Lady Washington. She'd been called "Lady" Washington since the Revolutionary War period. Martha called George "General" in public and "Papa" in private.

The picture we have of Martha Washington is that of a stately, plump woman. Her white hair frames a serene and cheerful face. She was usually dressed in a rather fancy, frilled cap and a simply cut gown. Abigail Adams wrote of Mrs. Washington in 1789 that "a most becoming pleasantness sits upon her countenance."

Even during the years in New York City, Martha was an early riser. And she always retired in the evening by nine o'clock. This habit drew considerable criticism. It meant that the first lady's evening entertainments always had to break up early. Guests had to leave when Martha announced that "the General retires at nine o'clock and I usually precede him. Good-night."

Society people in the young nation thought of themselves as sophisticated and cosmopolitan. But Martha's example seemed to discourage any kind of glittering nightlife.

During Washington's first year in office, he and Martha established a presidential custom. This was an annual New Year's Day open-house reception to which the public could come. Martha found such functions taxing but soon grew comfortable if not entirely pleased with her role as a public figure. The New Year's Day open house remained a custom at the White House until the time of Franklin Roosevelt.

Martha greatly resented the limitation placed upon members of the first family during the time they spent in

New York. Protocol forbade the first couple from accepting invitations to private homes. But they did enjoy some private outings. One of their favorites was the 14-mile drive by carriage around Manhattan Island. The Washingtons also enjoyed going to the theater.

The First Family Moves to Philadelphia

In 1790 the Washingtons moved to a larger home in New York City. It was a six-story house on Broadway, overlooking the Hudson River. They stayed there only a few months. By summertime, Congress had decided to move the government to Philadelphia. And the Washingtons had to move with the government. In all, the Washingtons lived in New York City a little more than a year.

The Washingtons arrived in Philadelphia in November. They rented a fine brick house away from the center of the city. The president's office was located on the third floor of the house. Robert and Marcia Morris were their landlords. They were also old friends.

Martha was much happier in Philadelphia than she had been in New York. In Philadelphia she could visit many of the people who had become her personal friends during the Revolutionary War. At that time, Philadelphia was the largest and liveliest city in the United States. It was a thriving place; prices were higher there than anywhere else.

Martha adopted the simple style of dress that was

popular among Quakers living there. Her dresses were always plain but of the best-quality fabric. Gloves were her one extravagance. She often bought dozens of pairs at a time.

The move to Philadelphia was only a temporary measure. A marvelous new city, soon to be named Washington, was being planned. It was, of course, south of Philadelphia, on the banks of the Potomac River. The city that was to become the nation's capital would have many splendid buildings. One of its most famous would be known as the White House. Beginning in 1800 the White House would be home to all presidential couples. But that was after the Washingtons. They were the only presidential family who never lived in this traditional home of the presidents.

The Washingtons' home in Philadelphia, the Robert Morris House on High Street

The First Family

George and Martha had no children of their own. When George married Martha, he raised Patty and Jack Custis as if they were his own. These children from Martha's first marriage became part of the first family. But both died relatively young.

Patty Custis was 17 when she died on June 19, 1773. George Washington had been about to leave Williamsburg. He was going to accompany John Murray, the new English governor, on a tour of Virginia's western frontier. But Martha's urgent message reached him in time. He was able to return to Mount Vernon for her last hours. Washington was at her bedside as Patty breathed her last. She had suffered all her life from epilepsy.

Jack Custis had lived a frivolous life until he decided to follow in Washington's footsteps and become a soldier. He enlisted as his stepfather's special aide. But he caught dysentery during the siege of Yorktown. The news reached Martha at Mount Vernon that Cornwallis had been taken. At the same time came the message that her son was near death. His last wish was to witness Cornwallis actually surrendering his sword. Jack was carried to the scene so that he could see this thrilling climax to the years of war. Then he was taken to Eltham Hall, a country estate some 30 miles away. At this home, which belonged to Martha's sister Nancy, he lingered four more days. This was enough time for his wife, Eleanor, and his mother to arrive to see him alive for the last time.

Although he was only 27 when he died, Jack left behind four children, a heavy burden for his young widow. George and Martha, who were now in their 50s, persuaded Jack's widow to let them raise the two youngest. They were named Eleanor (Nelly) and George Washington Parke Custis. The other two, five-year-old Eliza and four-year-old Martha, remained with their mother.

Nelly and her younger brother came to live at Mount Vernon, and they enlivened their grandparents' home. The Washingtons tried not to spoil their adopted children. Martha's niece, Fanny Bassett, was a frequent guest at Mount Vernon. She recalled that the children were constantly being reminded to be quiet and not to run in the house.

Vain as a child, Nelly grew into a gracious beauty. And young Washington showed much the same lack of discipline displayed by his father. He was a reluctant scholar and not much interested in education. He attended Princeton briefly before transferring to St. John's College in Annapolis, Maryland. He stayed there only a few months.

The talents displayed by young Nelly were carefully nurtured. Examples of her artwork still hang at Mount Vernon. These include a painting of a bird sitting on a cherry branch. Another example of Nelly's talent is a pair of silhouettes of George and Martha Washington. Nelly could also sing a little and play the harpsichord. Nelly's harpsichord, specially ordered by Washington in 1793 from London, still graces the parlor at Mount Vernon.

One of the comforts of Washington's old age was seeing Nelly settled and married. Fortunately Nelly gave birth to her first child several weeks before George Washington died. This knowledge helped cheer his final illness.

A famous portrait of the Washingtons at home was painted between 1789 and 1796 by Edward Savage. A relaxed George and Martha sit at a table with Nelly and young Washington standing next to them. A small black dog lies comfortably curled up on the map that the Washingtons seem to be examining, while a servant stands behind Martha's chair.

Washington playing the flute, accompanied by his step-daughter Nellie Custis

The Second Term

During Washington's first term in office, he managed to see that the Bill of Rights was passed. These were the first ten amendments to the Constitution. They protect Americans' basic liberties.

During his first term, there were no political parties as we now know them. But two parties were being developed. Thomas Jefferson stood for the Republicans. And Alexander Hamilton believed in *his* party, which he called the Federalists. It was not an easy time, and Washington was no longer a young man.

On March 4, 1793, George Washington was inaugurated for his second term as president. This time the whole family was there, including Martha, Nelly and little Washington. They were all present at Philadelphia's Federal Hall for the swearing-in ceremony. After a brief speech by Washington, Judge Cushing of the Supreme Court administered the oath of office.

In 1796 Congress pressured Washington to consider a third term. But by then he was an old man and not well. He flatly refused the offer. In the same year, Washington therefore prepared his Farewell Address. It was not delivered as a speech but was published in a Philadelphia newspaper. In March 1797 he and Martha said good-bye to public life.

Mount Vernon, the home of George and Martha Washington

The Last Years

John Adams succeeded Washington as president in 1796. His wife was Abigail Adams. She said of George Washington: "If we look through the whole tenor of his life, history will not produce to us a parallel."

The Washingtons returned to Mount Vernon. George was able to enjoy only about three years of peaceful retirement overlooking the Potomac. Life mostly revolved around the old General's comfort and convenience.

After taking a chill while riding over his estate in snow and sleet, Washington developed a throat infection. Two days later, on December 14, 1799, shortly after 10 P.M., he died. Martha had been at his side all day.

Congress wanted Washington's body to be interred in a special tomb in the new Capitol building in Washington, but Martha's wishes prevailed. She knew that her husband had wanted to be buried at Mount Vernon. And so Washington was buried in a simple brick mausoleum that he himself had designed. Martha kept a lock of her husband's hair as a keepsake. She carried it with her until her own death.

George Washington's will stated that when he and Martha were dead, the slaves at Mount Vernon would be freed. But Martha had already freed many of the slaves before she died.

Martha hated life in the public eye. To assure privacy after she and George were dead, Martha burned nearly all of the correspondence between herself and her husband. Still, in a letter preserved by her niece, Mrs. Washington confided, "I think I am more like a state prisoner than anything else, there is . . . certain bounds set for me which I must not depart from."

After George's death, Martha stayed more and more to herself. At times she believed her servants were plotting to kill her. She took little interest in life and spent much time in the smallroom she had fitted up for herself on the third floor of the main house at Mount Vernon. On May 22, 1802, she died after a few days of severe fever. She was buried beside her husband.

For Further Reading

Anthony, Carl Sferrazza. *First Ladies: The Saga of the Presidents' Wives and Their Power, 1789–1961.* New York: William Morrow and Company, Inc., 1990.

Fisher, Leonard Everett. *The White House.* New York: Holiday House, 1989.

Friedel, Frank. *The Presidents of the United States of America.* Revised edition. Washington, D.C.: The White House Historical Association, 1989.

Kinnaird, Clark. *George Washington, The Pictorial Biography.* New York: Hastings House, 1967.

Klapthor, Margaret Brown. *The First Ladies.* Revised edition. Washington, D.C.: The White House Historical Association, 1989.

Lindsay, Rae. *The Presidents' First Ladies.* New York: Franklin Watts, 1989.

The Living White House. Revised edition. Washington, D.C.: The White House Historical Association, 1987.

Meltzer, Milton. *George Washington and the Birth of Our Nation.* New York: Franklin Watts, 1986.

Menendez, Albert J. *Christmas in the White House*. Philadelphia: The Westminster Press, 1983.

St. George, Judith. *The White House: Cornerstone of a Nation*. New York: G. P. Putnam's Sons, 1990.

Siegel, Beatrice. *George and Martha Washington at Home in New York*. New York: Four Winds Press, 1989.

Index